I0480310

YOUR MONEY ISN'T
THE PROBLEM
YOUR MINDSET IS

Author/Editor: Rev. Darryl Bass

Electronic ISBN: 978-1-972115-09-1(EPUB)
978-1-972115-31-2 (Kindle)
Paperback ISBN: 978-1-972115-10-7
Hardcover ISBN: **978-1-972115-11-4**

Printed in the United States

The Library of Congress Control Number: 2026906572

Bass Publishing, LLC
Maywood, IL 60153

i

Disclaimer

The information contained in this book is for educational and informational purposes only. It is not intended as financial, legal, tax, medical, psychological, or professional advice. The author and publisher make no guarantees regarding the results that may be obtained from the use of this material.

All examples provided are illustrative and are not intended to represent or guarantee that any individual will achieve similar results. Personal growth, financial improvement, and life progression outcomes depend on individual effort, discipline, decisions, and circumstances.

Readers are encouraged to seek qualified professional advice regarding financial planning, legal matters, mental health, or other specialized areas before making decisions based on the information provided in this book.

The author and publisher disclaim any liability for any loss, risk, or damages, direct or indirect, that may arise from the use or application of the information contained herein.

By reading this book, you acknowledge that you are responsible for your own decisions, actions, and results.

Details in any stories and anecdotes have been changed to protect the identities of the person(s) involved.

Scripture quotations are taken from the King James Version of the Bible.

Dedication

To every person who has ever felt like they were doing all
they could,
and still came up short.

To the ones who gave, poured, served, sacrificed, and stood
strong
even when life was heavy on your shoulders.

To the ones who prayed quietly while carrying the weight
loudly.

To the ones who were taught how to survive,
but were never shown how to build.

This book is for you.

For the ones who decided:
"This cycle ends with me."

To my family, my children, and the generations that will come
after me — may you never have to fight the battles I had to
overcome. May you build from my healed places, not my
broken ones. May you inherit clarity, alignment, abundance,
and identity.

And to the Lord, who met me when I had nothing left but
faith — Thank You for showing me that breakthrough begins
in the mind long before it ever appears in the bank.

This is legacy.
This is freedom.
This is just the beginning.

— Rev. Darryl Bass

About the Author

 Reverend Darryl Bass is an author, teacher, pastor, and transformational coach dedicated to helping individuals and families build stronger lives spiritually, personally, and financially. With a background that includes service in the financial sector and years of ministry leadership, he brings together practical wisdom, real-world experience, and faith-centered insight to guide people toward lasting change.

As Assistant Pastor of Impact Church in Maywood, Illinois, Rev. Bass has committed his life to serving others with compassion, clarity, and purpose. His work extends far beyond the pulpit. He is known for empowering people through life coaching, financial education, spiritual encouragement, and systems designed to help individuals break cycles, gain direction, and build lasting stability.

Rev. Bass is also a devoted husband and father who deeply values faith, family, discipline, and legacy. His life and work reflect a commitment to helping people not only overcome present challenges, but also create a future marked by wisdom, stewardship, and generational impact.

An entrepreneur at heart, he has founded and developed multiple mission-driven ventures centered on financial literacy, debt freedom, personal growth, and community advancement. Through his teaching, writing, and program development, he has consistently focused on helping others improve their credit, increase income, eliminate debt, strengthen savings, prepare for retirement, and build a foundation that can bless future generations.

What sets Rev. Darryl Bass apart is his ability to connect principle with practice. His message is not merely about inspiration, but implementation. Whether writing about mindset, money, faith, legacy, or personal development, his goal is always the same: to equip people with the tools, wisdom, and confidence they need to move forward intentionally.

Through every book, Rev. Bass continues his mission of helping people rise above limitation, walk in purpose, and build lives that reflect both abundance and responsibility.

Contents

INTRODUCTION

You Were Never Meant to Struggle

There comes a moment in life where you have to stop and ask yourself,

"Why does this keep happening to me?"

Why do the bills feel heavier than the paycheck?
Why does money slip away faster than it comes in?
Why does peace feel like something you *visit* and never something you *live in*?

Why does it seem like no matter how hard you work,
how much you pray,
how much you care,
how much you sacrifice…

Life still pulls you back into the same financial cycles?

It's not because you're lazy.
It's not because you're irresponsible.

It's not because God is withholding something from you.

And it's **certainly not** because you're cursed.

Most of us were simply **never taught how to think about money.**

We inherited survival habits from people who were doing the best they could with what they had. We watched hard-working parents stretch pennies into meals and miracles into months.
We learned how to be strong, how to endure, how to pray, how to push…

But nobody taught us how to **build**.
How to structure.
How to multiply.
How to create stability.
How to turn income into impact.
How to break cycles instead of repeat them.

We were trained to **survive**, not to **live**.

And survival is a mindset — not a season.

If the mind remains in survival mode, the money will always mirror it.
Your finances can't outgrow your thinking.

This is the truth most people never hear:

Your money is not the problem.
Your mindset is.

Money only follows the identity holding it.
Your life cannot rise above the story you believe about yourself.
Your bank account cannot expand beyond your self-worth.
Your financial capacity cannot exceed your mental capacity.

You will never walk in what you do not believe you are worthy to carry.

This book is not about blame.
It is not about shame.
It is not about dwelling on the past.

This book is about **awakening.**

This book is about:

- Understanding the beliefs that shaped you
- Healing the emotions that have been driving your decisions
- Breaking the cycles that have lived in your bloodline
- And stepping into the identity God intended when He formed you

This book is about reclaiming:

- Your strength
- Your clarity
- Your power
- Your vision
- Your legacy

You are not broken.
You are not behind.
You are not less than.
You are not disqualified.

You are simply **becoming**.

And becoming requires a mental shift —
a reintroduction to your true self.

The self that God sees.
The self your future is waiting for.

The self your purpose recognizes.
The self that was never meant to struggle, but to **steward**.

Take a breath.

You are standing at the threshold of identity transformation.
Not just financial improvement — **internal elevation**.

Your life is about to rise.

Because now… you are ready.

CHAPTER ONE: The Mindset Trap: Why Most People Stay Stuck.

There are people who will work their entire lives — good people, praying people, loving people, strong people — and still never experience the financial peace they long for. Not because they were lazy. Not because they lacked intelligence. Not because they didn't *want* better.

But because **no one ever taught them how to think differently**.

We were raised in environments where **survival was the culture**.
Where "making it" meant *getting by*, not rising up.
Where stress was normal.
Where lack was familiar.
Where pressure was inherited.

And anything that becomes familiar begins to feel **true**, even when it's not.

Most of us didn't grow up with wealth — we grew up with **worry**.

We watched our parents stretch food, stretch bills, stretch patience.
We learned to make do, adjust, "keep it moving," and smile through tears.
We learned to look strong while silently drowning.

But listen, Rev — **survival is not your identity.**
Survival was only the *season* that introduced you to God's strength.

The problem is when survival becomes a **mindset**.

Because once survival becomes your mindset, you begin to believe:

- Money is always hard to get
- Struggle is normal
- Good things are temporary
- Opportunities are risky
- You have to work twice as hard for half the result
- You should be grateful just to have "enough"

And that mindset builds your financial ceiling.

Not your income.
Not your job.
Not your background.

Your **mindset**.

The Four Levels of Living

There are four financial dimensions' people occupy:

1. **Survival** – "I just need enough to make it through today."
2. **Stability** – "My bills are paid, but that's about it."
3. **Success** – "I have overflow and the ability to move forward."
4. **Significance** – "My wealth is now building legacy for others."

Most people are stuck at **Level One** or **Level Two,** not because they lack desire…
but because their **mind never learned to imagine Levels Three and Four as normal.**

You cannot walk into a room you cannot first **see** in your mind.

You cannot live a life your identity does not believe you deserve.

You cannot receive on the outside what you have rejected on the inside.

Your life will always rise — or fall — to the level of your self-perception.

The Invisible Cage

The enemy doesn't have to block your blessings if he can block your **perspective**.

If he can convince you:

- That increase is unrealistic for you
- That wealth is "for other people"
- That your background disqualifies you
- That your mistakes make you unworthy
- That your story is too broken

Then he never has to touch your bank account —
your mind will limit your life for him.

Financial bondage begins where **mental bondage** lives.

This is the trap.
Not the bills.
Not the career.
Not the economy.

The trap is the mindset.

But here's the good news:

A mindset is not permanent.
It is moldable.
Trainable.
Transformable.

You can **re-teach your mind** what is possible.
You can **recondition your identity** to align with abundance.
You can **break patterns** that have lasted generations.

And once your mind shifts — your money will begin to follow.

Because **your finances are the echo of your beliefs.**
Change the belief → The echo changes.

Take a moment.
Let your soul acknowledge this truth:

The life I desire is not out of reach —
it's locked inside a mindset I have not yet
mastered.

And today... the lock is coming loose.

CHAPTER TWO: The Wounds Behind Your Wallet

Money is not just math.
Money is **emotional.**
Money is **spiritual.**
Money is **psychological.**
Money is tied to **who you believe you are**
and **what you believe you deserve.**

Before we ever make a financial decision with
our **hands**, we make one with our **heart**.

This is why two people can receive the same
amount of money…
One builds from it — the other breaks from
it.
One multiplies — the other mismanages.
One sees seed — the other sees stress.
One sees opportunity — the other sees
obligation.

The difference isn't income.
The difference is **internal programming**.

Let's talk about it.

The Financial Trauma We Don't Discuss

There are wounds you can *see* — and then there are wounds that live **quietly** behind the eyes:

- Watching the lights get cut off
- Hearing grown folks argue about bills
- Sharing food to stretch meals
- Wearing clothes that weren't bought with you in mind
- Seeing your parents give up their dreams just to keep the family going

You don't forget those things.
Not because they were dramatic — but because they were **formational**.

When a child watches chaos around money, the child is silently learning:

"Money is stressful."
"Money is hard to manage."
"Money causes conflict."
"Money breaks peace."
"Money is unpredictable."

Without realizing it, you grew up with a **negative emotional relationship with money**, even when you didn't mean to.

So now as an adult:

- Money comes in → you feel anxious.
- Money leaves → you feel fear.
- Money grows → you feel undeserving.
- Money is discussed → you feel pressure.

Not because you're irresponsible…
But because your **heart never healed from what your childhood survived**.

Your spending is not disobedience.
Your saving is not inconsistency.
Your inconsistent financial habits are **symptoms of old wounds**.

And we don't condemn symptoms.
We **heal the source**.

The Pressure to Look Blessed

We live in a culture that taught us how to **perform** success before we ever learned how to **build** it.

We learned:

- How to look strong while hurting
- How to dress like we have money while struggling
- How to celebrate publicly while crying privately

Some of us didn't buy clothes, cars, vacations, or designer labels because we wanted them... We bought them because we wanted **relief**.

Relief from:

- Feeling "behind"
- Feeling overlooked
- Feeling unworthy
- Feeling like "everybody else" was ahead

Instead of healing the wound, we covered it with a purchase.

But every time you buy identity — the identity fades.
Every time you buy worthiness — the worth vanishes.
Every time you buy confidence — the confidence evaporates.

Because **money can buy the outfit but it cannot repair the self-image.**

There is **nothing wrong** with nice things. We are Kingdom. Excellence is our standard. But **excellence becomes bondage when it replaces identity.**

The Wound You Never Named

This is the truth that shifts everything:

Your spending is not about the item.

Your spending is about the *emotion attached* to the item.

You weren't buying the purse —
You were buying a sense of *being seen.*

You weren't buying the shoes —
You were buying a moment of *feeling valuable.*

You weren't buying the car —
You were buying *proof* that you were doing okay.

But let me say this with love and authority:

**You do not have to prove your worth.
You already carry it.**

Your identity is not purchased — it is *inherited*.
And your inheritance is **Kingdom.**

The Shift begins Here:

We are not just going to:

- Change your finances
- We are going to **heal your financial identity**.

This chapter is the moment the chains begin to loosen.
Not because of information — but because of **revelation.**

You are not wounded anymore.
You are awakening.

CHAPTER THREE: The Lies You Were Taught About Money

There are few subjects more misunderstood, more misquoted, more mishandled — than money.

And not just in the world.
But in our **homes**, in our **cultures**, and yes — even in our **churches**.

Most of the financial struggle people face is not because they lack opportunity, ability, or desire — it is because they were **trained to see money incorrectly**.

Let's expose the lies.

Because **what you believe determines what you allow.**

LIE #1: "Money Is the Root of All Evil."

This is one of the most misquoted scriptures in the Bible.

The actual verse says:

*"For the **love** of money is the root of all kinds of evil."*
— 1 Timothy 6:10

Not **money** — the *worship* of money.
Not **resources** — the *idolatry* of resources.

God does not hate wealth. (1 Timothy 6:17)
God **creates** wealth. (Deuteronomy 8:18)
God **transfers** wealth. (Proverbs 13:22)
God **instructs** wealth. (Psalm 32:8 and James 1:5)

God gave Abraham wealth. (Genesis 13:2)
God multiplied Isaac's fields. (Genesis 26:12–13)
God elevated Joseph to manage the wealth of nations. (Genesis 41:39–41)
God instructed Solomon in financial wisdom. (1 Kings 3:10–12 and 1 Kings 10:23–24)

So if God hated wealth, why would He place it in the hands of the righteous?

The problem is not money.
The problem is when money becomes **master** instead of **tool**.

LIE #2: "Rich People Are Greedy."

No — **greedy people are greedy.**
Money does not change character — it **reveals** it.

If you are generous with a little, you will be generous with much.
If you are selfish with a little, you will be selfish with much.

Money amplifies identity — it does not create it.

This is why God shapes **heart** before He releases **increase**.

Not to deprive you…
but to prepare you.

Because wealth in the hands of an unhealed person becomes **destructive,**
but wealth in the hands of a healed believer becomes **kingdom expansion.**

LIE #3: "God Wants Me Humble and Struggling."

Humility has nothing to do with poverty. Humility is not the absence of wealth — it is the absence of **pride**.

To believe God desires you broke is to believe God desires you **bound**.
And that is not scripture.
That is not gospel.
That is not Kingdom.

Jesus did not come so you could **survive**.
He came so you could have **life, and life more abundantly**.

Abundance is not arrogance.
Abundance is alignment.

Struggle is not spiritual.
Wisdom is spiritual.
Stewardship is spiritual.
Provision is spiritual.

LIE #4: "We Don't Talk About Money in This House."

That silence was not spiritual — it was **generational dysfunction**.

Families went decades refusing to talk about:

- What money is
- How to grow it
- How to manage it
- How to protect it
- How to multiply it

And because **no one talked**, no one learned.

You cannot heal what you refuse to **bring into the light**.

This book is the **light**.

LIE #5: "This Is Just How Life Is for People Like Us."

This is the lie that has kept more families bound than any credit card, any generational debt, any paycheck cycle.

"This is just how it is…"

No.
"This is how it *was*."
And **you are the interruption.**

You are the **disruptor.**
You are the **first to break it.**
You are the **first to shift it.**
You are the **one your bloodline has been praying for.**

What others survived — you will **transform.**
What they endured — you will **end.**
What they accepted — you will **rewrite.**

Your lineage is being rewritten **through you.**

Truth to Replace the Lies

- Wealth is not sinful — **it is stewardship.**
- Money is not to be worshiped — **it is to be managed.**
- God does not bless greed — **He blesses purpose.**
- Poverty is not holy — **clarity is holy. Discipline is holy. Alignment is holy.**

And when your **mind aligns with truth**, your **money aligns with destiny.**

CHAPTER FOUR: Your Self-Image Sets Your Financial Ceiling

You cannot out-earn your identity.
You cannot out-build your belief system.
You cannot out-run the image you hold of yourself.

If a person believes they are:

- Unworthy of increase
- Unqualified for overflow
- Destined for struggle
- Or "the one who always has to fight for everything"

Then even when opportunity arrives…
even when doors open…
even when God *answers*…

They will sabotage what was meant to bless them.

Not because they're broken.
Not because they're weak.

But because their **internal self-image** does not match the **external possibility**.

Your life will never expand beyond the boundaries your mind has drawn around it.

The Inner Blueprint

Every person walks around with a **financial blueprint** — a silent, subconscious framework built from:

- Childhood experiences
- Family patterns
- Cultural beliefs
- Religious interpretations
- Emotional wounds
- Social influence

This blueprint determines what feels:

- Normal
- Comfortable
- Familiar
- Safe

Even if "normal" is struggle.
Even if "familiar" is stress.
Even if "safe" is survival.

So when God tries to elevate you — your blueprint pulls you back.

Not out of rebellion…
but out of **conditioning**.

Your life will always return to the level of your **internal "home."**

That's why some people earn more and still feel broke.
That's why some get raises and still stay behind.
That's why some get tax refunds and still end up depleted.

The problem was never money.
The problem was the **internal temperature** of identity.

The Spiritual Principle:
Your Mind Must Match What You're Praying For

You cannot pray for overflow while your mind is still loyal to lack.

You cannot declare abundance while your self-worth whispers:

"I'm not good enough."

You cannot give expecting harvest if you still believe:

"Increase is for other people."

God does not put new wine into old
wineskins.
Not because He withholds,
but because **He protects.**

If He gives you more while your self-image is
still wounded —
the blessing will become a burden.

So He transforms **you** first.

The Way You See You Matters

Listen to this:

**If you see yourself as a survivor, you will always have something to survive.
If you see yourself as a struggler, you will always have something to struggle with.
If you see yourself as the one who "makes it is through," you will never step into overflow.**

Identity dictates reality.

So the transformation begins here:

Who are you?

Not your job.
Not your income.
Not your mistakes.
Not your history.

Who **are you?**

Because the moment you begin to see yourself as:

- Chosen

- Worthy
- Called
- Equipped
- Capable
- Anointed
- Designed for dominion

Your money will rise to meet the version of you God has always known you to be.

This is Your Self-Image Shift

Repeat this — slowly — with intention:

I am not here to survive.
I am here to build.
I am not here to chase money.
Money is assigned to me.
I do not live in lack.
I live in alignment.
I am worthy of overflow.
I am trusted with increase.
I am called to steward abundance.
This is who I am.
And this is who I will be.

CHAPTER FIVE: Discipline Is a Spiritual Act

Most people think discipline is about restriction.
But discipline is not punishment —
discipline is positioning.

Discipline is how you *prepare* for what you prayed for.

You can't ask God for **increase** and keep the habits of **lack**.
You can't ask God for **wealth** and remain loyal to financial chaos.
You can't ask God for **overflow** while living with open leaks in your stewardship.

Breakthrough is not just **what God sends** —
Breakthrough is **what you are positioned to sustain.**

And discipline is the difference.

Disorder is Expensive

A disordered financial life drains:

- Time
- Energy
- Peace
- Confidence
- Future stability

Chaos has a cost.

And many have paid that cost for years — not because they were irresponsible —
but because **no one ever taught them the spiritual side of order**.

But hear this clearly:

Order is a language heaven responds to.

Whenever God prepares to bless something, the first thing He brings is **structure**.

Look at Genesis:

- The earth was formless → **God brought order**
- Then came **increase, propagation**, and **multiplication**

Where there is **order**, there can be **overflow.**

Where there is **structure**, there can be **sustained blessing.**

Where there is **discipline**, there can be **dominion.**

Self-Control is a Form of Self-Respect

The enemy wants you impulsive. Why?

Because impulsive people are predictable people.
And predictable people are **controllable**.

But disciplined people?
They are dangerous.
Because they can't be moved by:

- Emotion
- Temptation
- Pressure
- Comparison

Discipline breaks the cycle of emotional spending.
Discipline silences the need to "look blessed."
Discipline ends the constant chaos of financial emergencies.

Discipline is not the enemy of freedom —
Discipline is the doorway to freedom.

The Spirituality of Budgeting

Say this with me:

A budget is not bondage — a budget is boundaries.

A budget is not God saying "no."
A budget is *you* saying:

- "This is where my money will go."
- "This is what aligns with my future."
- "This honors my purpose."
- "This protects my peace."

A budget is faith in written form:

- Faith that overflow is coming
- Faith that increase is intentional
- Faith that wealth is a process, not an accident

Budgeting is not about living less.
It's about **becoming more.**

The Holy Gift of Delayed Gratification

People who cannot delay what they desire
will always live dependent on what they have.

But listen to this revelation:

Your future is worth waiting for.
Your peace is worth preserving.
Your legacy is worth protecting.

You don't need the blessing *fast*.
You need the blessing to *last*.

And lasting blessings are built with discipline.

Discipline is a Declaration

Every time you:

- Say no to unnecessary spending
- Say yes to saving
- Pay off debt with intention
- Set financial boundaries
- Walk past something you want because
  you're choosing something greater…

You are declaring to the world and to your own soul:

"I am in control. My future is not being traded for temporary feelings."

This.
Is.
Spiritual.
Maturity.

This is Where Your Life Begins to Rise

Discipline is how you move from:

- Survival → Stability
- Stability → Success
- Success → Significance

Not overnight.
Not in panic.
But in **purpose**.

Your destiny is not waiting on more money.
Your destiny is waiting on **alignment**.

And alignment begins with discipline.

CHAPTER SIX: How to Break the Cycle of Financial Struggle

Cycles don't break because you *want* them to break.
Cycles break because you **interrupt** them.

Struggle is not just a financial condition — it is a **repeated pattern**:

- The same habits
- The same reactions
- The same emotional triggers
- The same spending behaviors
- The same survival decisions

Over and over again.

You are not just fighting numbers —
You are confronting **patterns that have been passed down**, rehearsed, normalized, and accepted as "just life."

But this time, the cycle ends.
Not by accident — but by **intention**.

The Three-Stage Breakthrough Process

1. AWARENESS – *See the pattern*

2. ALIGNMENT – *Replace the pattern*

3. ACTION – *Reinforce the new pattern*

This is how transformation becomes **permanent**, not temporary.

Let's walk through each step.

STEP 1: AWARENESS

You cannot change what you refuse to confront.

This is the moment where you look at your life without shame, without excuses, without guilt — and simply **tell the truth.**

Write this somewhere:

"My finances are a reflection of my patterns, not my potential."

Potential has never been the issue.
Your ability has never been the issue.
Your future has never been the issue.

The *pattern* was the issue.

Awareness is not condemnation.
Awareness is empowerment.
Once you see the pattern, **it loses power over you.**

STEP 2: ALIGNMENT

Your habits must match your future.

Alignment is where you stop living by emotion, impulse, and reaction —
and start living by **design**.

This is where you:

- Decide who you are becoming
- Decide where you are going
- Decide what your life will look like
- Decide how your money will be assigned

Alignment is the death of autopilot.

From now on, every dollar has a purpose.
Every choice has a meaning.
Every decision has a direction.

You are no longer reacting to life.
You are *designing* it.

STEP 3: ACTION

Change is not real until behavior shifts.

Information inspires.
Revelation awakens.
But **action transforms.**

Here is where the cycle breaks:

You do the opposite of what the old version of you would have done.

- When you want to spend → **you pause.**
- When you feel impulsive → **you breathe.**
- When you feel pressured to "prove something" → **you remind yourself: I am already enough.**

- When your emotions rise → **you sit in stillness until clarity returns.**

This is how cycles collapse.

Not with force.
But with **new choices**, made consistently.

Breaking the Cycle Looks Like This:

- You stop buying relief — and start building restoration
- You stop chasing moments — and start planning futures
- You stop reacting to money — and start instructing money
- You stop proving your worth — and start protecting it

This is *maturity*.
This is *stewardship*.
This is *identity in action*.

The Enemy Doesn't Fear Your Income

He fears your **discipline**.
He fears your **clarity**.
He fears your **alignment**.

Because once you become consistent —
you become **dangerous.**

Cycles break when you stop living from
emotion
and start living from **vision**.

Declaration

Speak this aloud:

**I break every financial cycle that has lived
in my family.
I break every mindset that kept me in
survival.
I choose clarity.
I choose order.
I choose discipline.
I choose wealth as identity, not accident.
My life is shifting.
My lineage is changing.
This cycle ends with me.**

CHAPTER SEVEN: Wealth Is Not a Number, It's a Culture

Most people think wealth is about how much money you have.
But wealth is not a dollar amount.
Wealth is a **way of thinking.**
A way of **moving.**
A way of **stewarding.**
A way of **seeing the world.**

Wealth is a **culture.**

And culture is not what you do *once.*
Culture is what you do **consistently**.

This is why someone can win the lottery and be broke again in two years.
They **received wealth**, but they **never became wealthy.**

Money can increase quickly —
but identity must be built **intentionally**.

Wealth Thinks in Investment, not Impulse

Poor thinking says:

"How fast can I spend this?"

Middle-class thinking says:

"How can I look like I'm doing well?"

Wealth thinking says:

"How can I multiply this?"

Wealthy people don't ask:

- "What can I buy?"

They ask:

- "What can I *build*?"

Because they know:
Money is not the goal — money is the tool.

And those who master the tool shape the world.

Wealthy People Plan with Purpose

Most people live in reaction:

- Reacting to bills
- Reacting to emergencies
- Reacting to pressure
- Reacting to income changes

Wealthy people live in **intention**:

- They schedule their future
- They project expenses
- They assign money to purpose
- They let vision make decisions

Wealth is not chaotic — it's **organized.**

Order attracts increase.
Structure sustains blessing.
Planning multiplies resources.

This is why the enemy fights your ability to plan —
because planning is **prophetic.**

Wealthy People Value Time Differently

Poor thinking says:

"I'll do it when I have time."

Wealth thinking says:

"I schedule time for what matters."

Because wealthy people know:
Time is more expensive than money.
Money spent can be replaced.
Time spent **never returns.**

So they:

- Protect their energy
- Decline unnecessary commitments
- Simplify their environment
- Automate what can be automated
- Delegate what someone else can do

Their peace is not negotiable.
Their focus is not on sale.
Their purpose is not available for distraction.

This is not arrogance.
This is **alignment.**

Wealthy People Build Systems

A poor mindset works *hard*.
A wealthy mindset works **intentionally**.

A wealthy person doesn't ask:

- "How can *I* do this forever?"

They ask:

- "How can I build a **system** that does this for me?"

Systems:

- Multiply time
- Multiply money
- Multiply impact
- Multiply peace

If you have to be present for everything to work — it's not wealth.
It's **overwork disguised as achievement.**

Wealth requires **systems**.

THE SHIFT HAPPENS WHEN THIS TRUTH SINKS IN:

I am not building income — I am building identity.

Once you see yourself as:

- Strategic
- Disciplined
- Purpose-driven
- Consistent
- Focused
- Trustworthy with increase

Your life will **rise to match** that identity.

Because wealth begins in the **mind,**
moves into **habits,**
and results in **outcomes.**

Declaration of Alignment

Say this with boldness:

I think like a builder.
I plan like a leader.
I steward like a king.
Money is not my master — it is my instrument.
I am trusted with increase.

I am aligned with overflow.
I am becoming who wealth already sees
me as.

CHAPTER EIGHT: Developing a Prosperity Mindset

Prosperity is not about having more —
it is about becoming more.

It is a posture of the mind,
a position of the spirit,
and a rhythm of expectation.

Prosperity is a **language,**
a **lens,**
and a **lifestyle.**

It is not loud or boastful.
It does not have to announce itself.
Prosperity moves **quietly**, confidently, and
consistently.

Prosperity is **peaceful.**

Because prosperity begins with **inner
alignment**, not outer acquisition.

The Language of Prosperity

People living in lack talk from:

- Limitations
- Fear
- Scarcity
- Pressure

They speak in survival phrases like:
"Hopefully."
"We'll see."
"I'm just trying to get by."
"It always goes wrong."
"I never have enough."

But those with a prosperity mindset speak from:

- Truth
- Faith
- Strategy
- Identity
- Stability

They speak differently:

"There is always a way."
"God has gone before me."
"I am graced for increase."
"Money serves my purpose."
"I am trusted with abundance."

Because **your mouth shapes your reality**. Your words reveal what your mind believes is possible.

When your language shifts, your life shifts.

The Posture of Prosperity

A prosperity mindset is **rooted**, not reactive.

You don't chase blessings — blessings **recognize you**.

You don't run after opportunities — opportunities **look for your consistency**.

You don't panic when there is a delay — because **delay does not mean denial** when you're aligned.

A prosperous person moves like someone who:

- Knows they are called
- Knows they are prepared
- Knows increase is inevitable
- Knows doors will open

- Knows what is coming cannot be stopped

There is **rest** in prosperity.

Not laziness.
Not passivity.
Rest.

Rest is the evidence of trust.

The Patience of Prosperity

People with a prosperity mindset understand:

Wealth doesn't respond to urgency — it responds to consistency.

Anyone can be excited for a week.
Anyone can budget for a month.
Anyone can declare for a season.

But prosperity belongs to those who:

- Keep doing the small things well
- Honor their commitments to themselves
- Hold their identity steady during waiting
- Remain unshaken during transition

The prosperous are not the quickest —
they are the **most consistent.**

Stability is the soil of abundance.

The Alignment Check

Ask yourself:

- Do I speak like someone who expects increase?
- Do I plan like someone who is building legacy?
- Do I carry myself like someone trusted with wealth?
- Do I live like my future is already secured in God?

If the answer is **no** — don't feel guilt.
Feel **opportunity.**

This is a *becoming.*
Not a performance.
Not a competition.

A becoming.

The Shift begins with Agreement

Say this, — and feel the weight of it:

I am not trying to earn abundance.
I am aligning with abundance.
I do not chase money.
Money locates purpose.
I am prepared for increase.
I expect overflow.
Prosperity is normal for me.
This is who I am.

Yes.

Let it settle.

Your mind is shifting.

Your identity is rising.

Your capacity is expanding.

CHAPTER NINE: Money Flows Where Purpose Goes

Money is not attracted to desire.
Money is not attracted to need.
Money is not attracted to struggle.

Money is attracted to **purpose.**

Where there is **clarity of assignment,** there will always be **provision for the assignment.**

This is why some people can work endlessly and feel stuck, while others step into alignment and watch resources begin to move. Not because God plays favorites — but because **God funds purpose.**

God does not finance identity crises.
But He will always finance **vision.**

The Danger of Chasing Money

When you chase money, you are always:

- Tired
- Frustrated

- Overworked
- Inconsistent
- Emotionally drained

Because chasing money is **rooted in fear**, and anything rooted in fear is unstable.

Fear says:

"If I don't hurry, I'll miss it."

"If I don't grab it now, I'll never get another chance."

But purpose says:

"What is for me cannot be taken from me. I do not chase. I *become*."

Money is a **follower**, not a leader.

When you pursue money, you lose yourself. When you pursue purpose, money **finds you**.

Your Gifts were not Random

There are things you do so naturally you assume they don't matter:

- The way you speak life
- The way you solve problems
- The way you encourage people
- The way you strategize
- The way you break things down for others
- The way you create order out of chaos

You thought that was just personality.

No, that was **blueprint**.

God hid **business models in your compassion.**
He hid **wealth in your creativity.**
He hid **impact in your intellect.**
He hid **legacy in your voice.**

Your calling is not accidental — it is **assigned.**

And what is assigned is always **resourced.**

When Purpose Speaks, Provision Responds

When you step into identity…
When you step into clarity…

When you step into the work God formed you to do…

Something begins to shift around you.

People will **start finding you.**
Opportunities will **start opening.**
Resources will **start aligning.**
Doors that never opened before will **swing wide.**

Not because "luck changed" —
but because **purpose took the stage.**

Purpose is a magnet.
Purpose pulls what is required for its fulfillment.

The Questions that Changes Everything

Instead of asking:

- "How do I make more money?"

Ask:

- **"What has God assigned me to build?"**

Instead of asking:

- "How do I get paid?"

Ask:

- **"Who am I called to serve?"**

Purpose always lives in:

- Who you lift
- Who you heal
- Who you help
- Who you lead
- Who you empower

Money is the echo.
Purpose is the voice.

When the voice speaks, the echo follows.

The Shift in Your Soul

Say this:

**My life is not random.
My calling is not accidental.
I have been equipped for the people I am assigned to.
Money does not lead me — purpose leads me.
And provision follows purpose.
I walk in clarity.
I walk in confidence.
I walk in calling.**

Amen.

CHAPTER TEN: Walking Boldly into Your New Financial Identity

You have learned.
You have confronted.
You have healed.
You have shifted.
You have awakened.

But now —
You must **become.**

Because revelation means nothing without embodiment.
Knowledge means nothing without identity.
Breakthrough means nothing without *movement.*

This chapter is not about learning something new.
This chapter is about **becoming someone new.**

Not a new personality.
Not a new image.
Not a new performance.

A **new identity** — One that has been waiting on you since the moment God formed you.

You Are No Longer Who You Were

The person who struggled is gone.
The person who feared lack is gone.
The person who reacted to money is gone.
The person who lived in survival is gone.

You are stepping into the version of yourself that God *created*.

The version that:

- Thinks clearly
- Moves intentionally
- Plans with purpose
- Speaks with authority
- Gives with confidence
- Builds with discipline
- Lives with peace

You are not becoming wealthy.
You are **remembering that you were always called to be so.**

Your Future has been Waiting for This Version of You

Every breakthrough you prayed for, cried for, labored for, believed for —
was always connected to the moment you would **decide:**

I am no longer living small.
I am no longer repeating cycles.
I am no longer shrinking to fit rooms I've outgrown.
I am no longer apologizing for being called.

Your future does not need a perfect version of you.
It needs a **committed** version of you.

Committed to:

- Growth
- Structure
- Healing
- Legacy
- Identity
- Purpose
- Discipline
- Destiny

Not perfectly.
But faithfully.

Your Environment Must Match Your New Identity

You cannot expect abundance to thrive where scarcity is still being entertained.

This means:

- Some conversations must change
- Some relationships must shift
- Some environments must be left
- Some habits must be released

Not in arrogance.
Not in judgment.

But because you cannot stay in rooms that were designed for the version of you who was surviving.

Your future requires **space**.

Create room for the person you are becoming.

The Daily Rewiring

Identity is not decided in a moment — it is reinforced daily.

Each day, you:

- Speak abundance
- Think with clarity
- Act with discipline
- Protect your peace
- Honor your purpose
- Steward your resources
- Align with what God has spoken over you

This is not performance.

This is **agreement**.

You are agreeing with:

- God's vision of you
- Heaven's assignment for you
- Your future's expectation of you

And agreement has power.

Declare this with Authority

Speak it slowly.
Speak it boldly.
Speak it until it becomes *memory* in your bones:

I am chosen for wealth.
I am trusted with abundance.
I am disciplined.
I am strategic.
I am aligned.
I am consistent.
I am increasing in wisdom, stature, and favor.
Money does not rule me — I govern it.
I walk in purpose.

I build legacy.
I honor God with my stewardship.
I am becoming who I was always destined to be.

Now exhale.
This is your identity now.

The Shift is Complete — But the Journey Continues

This book was not closure.
This book was **activation**.

Your life from this point forward will not move by accident —
it will move by **intention**, by **faith**, and by **purpose**.

You are not going back to who you were.
Not after this.
Not after what you've seen within yourself.
Not after what God has confirmed in your spirit.

This is not the end of the story.

This is the **beginning of the becoming.**

CONCLUSION

This Was Never About Money — It Was About Identity

Take a breath.
Let these final words rest in your spirit.

Everything you read in these chapters was not
simply information —
It was **remembrance.**

A remembering of who you were before life
tried to convince you to shrink.
A remembering of what God whispered
before fear tried to silence you.
A remembering of your original design before
survival tried to redefine you.

This journey was never just about money.
Money was only the mirror.
Money was the reflection of an unseen truth:

**You were becoming someone you no
longer are.**

You were evolving.
You were stretching.
You were waking up.

This book did not introduce you to a new self

—

It **reintroduced you to the self that God always knew.**

The **healed** you.
The **aligned** you.
The **disciplined** you.
The **focused** you.
The **strategic** you.
The **confident** you.
The **anointed** you.
The **abundant** you.

You are not who struggle tried to shape.
You are not who survival tried to define.
You are not who fear tried to limit.

You are **who God spoke**,
who destiny confirmed,
who purpose kept calling.

Your life will never shrink again.
Your thinking will never go back into small spaces.

Your decisions will no longer be governed by fear, lack, or pressure.

You have seen too much.
You have learned too much.
You have awakened too much.

The Future You Build from Here Matters

Your family will feel this shift.
Your children will live in the fruit of this shift.
Your lineage will thank you for this shift.

You are not just breaking cycles.
You are **building legacy.**

Legacy that goes beyond:

- Bank accounts
- Investments
- Assets

Legacy that is rooted in:

- Wisdom
- Identity
- Confidence
- Stewardship
- Faith
- Purpose

Your descendants will **not** inherit the fear you fought.
They will inherit the **freedom you chose.**

The Journey Continues

As you leave these pages, remember this:

You do not need motivation — you are
already moved.
You do not need approval — you are already
appointed.
You do not need permission — you are
already chosen.

The only thing left now is **execution**.

Not perfectly.
Not forcefully.
But faithfully.

A little every day.
Steady.
Focused.
Aligned.
Committed.

Because the version of you that God called —
is the version of you the world has been
waiting to experience.

You are stepping into **significance** now.

Go build.
Go increase.
Go multiply.
Go steward.
Go serve.
Go become.

Your money was never the problem.
Your mindset was.

And now — that mindset is **renewed.**

Walk boldly into your new identity.

Your future is already expecting you.

Other Books by Rev. Darryl Bass

This Is Why You're Broke

A bold and unapologetic examination of the habits, beliefs, and financial behaviors that keep people trapped in cycles of struggle. This book confronts uncomfortable truths and replaces excuses with execution, helping readers shift from reactive spending to strategic wealth building.

Healing Your Financial Trauma

This book addresses the psychological and emotional roots of money struggles, helping readers break cycles, confront financial pain, and rebuild confidence and stability.

The Financial Identity Shift

A mindset-and-behavior reset that helps readers align who they are with how they handle money, transforming financial habits through identity-based discipline.

The Life Progression System

A comprehensive blueprint for intentional living, The Life Progression System guides readers through structured personal growth, goal alignment, mindset transformation, and legacy building. It equips individuals with practical tools to move from drifting through life to deliberately designing it.

The Life Progression System Workbook

A comprehensive blueprint for intentional living, The Life Progression System guides readers through structured personal growth, goal alignment, mindset transformation, and legacy building. It equips individuals with practical tools to move from drifting through life to deliberately designing it.

Financial Progression System

This book provides a step-by-step roadmap to financial stability and long-term wealth building. It teaches readers how to increase income, eliminate debt, build credit, create savings systems, and establish generational financial security.

Borrowed Futures

A wake-up call about the hidden costs of debt and financial shortcuts, showing readers how to escape debt cycles and build futures without financial bondage.

Life Insurance: The Gift of Life After Life

More than a policy explanation, this book reframes life insurance as a strategic wealth-building and legacy-protection tool. It educates families on how to use life insurance for income replacement, debt protection, estate planning, generational wealth transfer, and financial leverage.

The Intellectual Property Wealth Blueprint

A strategic guide to turning knowledge into income, this book teaches creators how to package ideas into books, courses, systems, and assets that generate scalable and recurring revenue streams.

The Intellectual Property Wealth Blueprint 2.0

Focused on licensing, certification, and legacy systems, this volume expands intellectual property into scalable enterprises that create long-term wealth and generational ownership structures.

The Debt Eliminator
Coming 2026

What if 2026 was the year everything changed?

What if this was the year you stopped surviving... and started building?
The year you stopped juggling bills... and started creating wealth?
The year debt stopped controlling your decisions?

The **Debt Eliminator** is not another budgeting class.
It is a structured financial transformation system designed to help individuals and families break free from consumer debt, rebuild financial confidence, and establish a foundation for long-term wealth.

This course was built for hardworking people who are tired of living paycheck to paycheck. It was created for families who want stability, not stress. It was designed for individuals who know they are capable of more—but need a system that works.

What the Debt Eliminator Will Teach You:

• How to eliminate consumer debt strategically and aggressively
• How to increase income without adding overwhelm
• How to rebuild and optimize your credit profile
• How to build savings while eliminating debt
• How to structure emergency funds and protection plans
• How to shift your financial identity from borrower to builder
• How to create systems that prevent debt from returning

This is not theory.
This is execution.

Through step-by-step modules, implementation tools, accountability structure, and real-life application, you will learn how to take control of your money instead of letting it control you.

Imagine waking up without financial anxiety.
Imagine having a plan.
Imagine watching your balances decrease and your confidence increase.
Imagine positioning your household for ownership, investing, and generational legacy.

That transformation begins in 2026.

The Debt Eliminator is more than a course.
It is a movement toward financial clarity, discipline, and freedom.

Get ready to break cycles.
Get ready to build stability.
Get ready to eliminate debt—permanently.

The Debt Eliminator — Launching 2026.

Join our waiting list Today!
https://savingssolution.org/join

The Financial Freedom Revolution Tour

Launching 2026

This is not a seminar.
This is not a motivational rally.
This is a financial awakening.

The **Financial Freedom Revolution Tour** is a live, high-impact experience designed to ignite transformation in individuals, families, entrepreneurs, and communities ready to break financial cycles and build generational stability.

For too long, people have been working harder but falling further behind. Income rises. Expenses rise. Stress rises. Yet true financial progress feels out of reach.

The Revolution changes that.

This national tour brings together powerful teaching, real strategy, live coaching, and structured execution plans that move attendees from confusion to clarity—and from debt to disciplined wealth-building.

What You'll Experience:

• A clear roadmap to financial stability and long-term wealth
• Step-by-step strategies for eliminating consumer debt
• Income growth frameworks and entrepreneurship positioning
• Credit optimization and financial leverage strategies
• Protection planning and legacy-building principles
• Live financial assessments and actionable implementation steps

• A mindset shift from survival thinking to ownership thinking

This is not inspiration without structure.
This is strategy with accountability.

The Financial Freedom Revolution Tour is built for families who want peace instead of pressure. For entrepreneurs who want profit with structure. For leaders who understand that financial stability is the foundation for community impact.

Imagine thousands gathered in one space—learning, planning, committing to real change.
Imagine leaving with a clear blueprint instead of just excitement.
Imagine knowing exactly what steps to take the next day.

This is more than an event.
It is a declaration that debt cycles end here.
It is a call to financial responsibility, ownership, and generational leadership.

Cities across the country will host this movement in 2026.

Seats will fill.
Lives will shift.
Legacies will be built.

The Financial Freedom Revolution Tour — Coming 2026.

This is the year you stop reacting to money
…and start commanding it.

The revolution begins with one decision.
https://savingssolution.org/tour

Follow on Social Media

Facebook

https://www.facebook.com/LPSCoach

Twitter

https://twitter.com/LPS_Coach

Instagram

https://www.instagram.com/lps_coach/

YouTube

https://www.youtube.com/@life_progression_system

TikTok

https://www.tiktok.com/@debt_annihilator

LinkedIn

https://www.linkedin.com/in/lpscoach/

SoundCloud

https://soundcloud.com/lps_coach

Pintrest

https://www.pinterest.com/LPS_Coach/